Victorian
Frozen Dainties

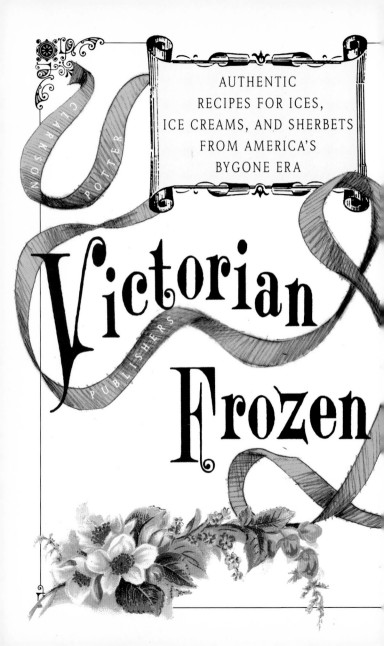

AUTHENTIC
RECIPES FOR ICES,
ICE CREAMS, AND SHERBETS
FROM AMERICA'S
BYGONE ERA

CLARKSON

POTTER

PUBLISHERS

Victorian

Frozen

Dainties

NEW YORK

ALLISON KYLE LEOPOLD

SPECIAL EDITORIAL CONSULTANT:
JOANNE LEONHARDT CASSULLO

Published by Clarkson N. Potter, Inc., 201 East 50th Street, New York,
New York 10022. Member of the Crown Publishing Group.
Random House, Inc. New York, Toronto, London, Sydney, Auckland

CLARKSON N. POTTER, POTTER, and colophon are trademarks of
Clarkson N. Potter, Inc.

Manufactured in Hong Kong

Design by Beth Tondreau Design / Mary A. Wirth

Library of Congress Cataloging-in-Publication Data

Leopold, Allison Kyle.
Victorian frozen dainties / by Allison Kyle Leopold.
p.   cm.
1. Ice cream, ices, etc.   2. Frozen desserts.   3. England—Social
life and customs—19th century.   I. Title.
TX795.L47   1994
641.8'62—dc20   92-30641
CIP

ISBN 0–517–59143–X

10 9 8 7 6 5 4 3 2 1

First Edition

CONTENTS

INTRODUCTION • 7

1 • VICTORIAN ICE CREAMS • 13

All-Purpose Victorian Ice Cream Bases
Bisque and Brown Bread Ice Cream
Burnt Almond Ice Cream and Other Nut Creams
Cucumber Ice Cream . . . Chestnut Ice Cream
Fruit Ice Creams . . . Gooseberry Ice Cream
Chocolate Ice Cream

2 • WATER ICES AND GRANITÉS • 33

Macedoine Ice
Lemon Water Ice and Ginger Water Ice
Strawberry Granité . . . Rose Ice
Red Currant Fruit Ice

3 • SHERBETS, MOUSSES, AND OTHER DELIGHTS • 45

Frozen Pudding . . . Violet Sherbet
Maple Parfait . . . Caramel Mousse . . . Apple Sorbet
Peach Bombe Glacé . . . Biscuit Princess

CONCORDANCE FOR MODERN COOKS • 60

HELPFUL HINTS ON MEASUREMENTS • 63

ACKNOWLEDGMENTS • 64

The Gem Freezer
The Best in the World.

To cook a heavy dinner in hot weather, to wash the dishes
afterward, this is sober prose, and by a very dull author;
but to make the dessert, this is poetry.
—M. E. W. Sherwood,
THE ART OF ENTERTAINING, 1893

INTRODUCTION

ome Victorian dishes are absurdly complicated, requiring daunting lists of obscure ingredients, as well as hours of tedious preparation, often to somewhat dubious result. But when it comes to the ices, ice creams, and frosty mousses that nineteenth-century Americans enjoyed at garden parties and birthday fêtes, at fancy dinners, picnics, and summer sociables, it's quite a different story. These frozen treats, flavored with the sweet natural juices of ripe berries and fruits, studded with nuts, and sometimes fragrant with wine, are among the most appealing and easily made desserts of the last century's table.

Many of these treats are distinctly different from those we buy today. The textures are more varied—from icy granités to slushy snows, melting rich custard-based creams, and thick, dense frozen mousses. And the flavors are intriguing, for while the Victorians had their versions of the basics—vanilla, chocolate, and strawberry—they also enjoyed innovative flavor combinations, making use of exotic fruits and nuts, French coffees, tea, and spices that were fashionable and accessible at the time. Clove flavoring was said to be popular in the East (though virtually nonexistent in the Midwest). Quince snow, exquisite violet sherbet (embellished with tiny candied violets), red currant fruit ice, fig ice cream—all were quintessential nineteenth-century creations.

Some Victorian flavors, however, while novel, may strike us as curious. The Victorian fondness for vegetable ice creams, made from asparagus, spinach, or celery, is one such curiosity. The novelty of cucumber ice cream, however, remains beguiling; decorated with a sprig of mint, it's an unexpectedly piquant refresher on a hot summer day.

Numerous cookbooks of the second half of the nineteenth century featured other singular combinations, revealing an appreciation of textures and tastes far more adventurous than is ours today. For example, the Victorians were partial to the mixing of molassesy brown bread crumbs into vanilla-based ice cream to create brown bread ice cream. Crumbling up stale macaroons, lady fingers, angel food cake, fruit or sponge cake, wine biscuits, graham wafers, or meringues into ice cream, often with a little sherry, produced the popular "bisque" flavors. These can be regarded as Victorian forerunners of today's "cookies-and-cream" ice creams or ice cream with "mix-ins."

All sorts of grand and elaborate molded ice creams and ices were also created. The hard work that went into their making was believed to demonstrate a homemaker's artistic sensibility and creativity, and the commendable ability to present guests with a dessert that was expensive (made with costly cream, eggs, and white sugar) and rare (things frozen retained an air of novelty well into the 1920s) as well as decorative and delicious. "There has never been a time like the present, when housekeepers gave so much attention to the appearance as well as to the palatableness of household cookery," said one Dr. V. C. Price, who billed himself as "the housewife's friend and pure food expert" in *Dr. Price's Delicious Desserts* (1904). "A love of daintiness is inherent in the heart of every true housewife, and when this can be gained without loss of health or comfort, a great boon has been conferred."

Extravagant molded ice cream "bombes" consisted of an outer layer of sherbet or ice cream concealing an inner surprise of a carefully chosen frozen filling, usually a mousse. "The handsomest dishes, of course, are made with the brightest colored sherbets," noted Maria Parloa, author of several immensely popular cookery books. She emphasized compatibility of flavors, noting that the outer layer tended to absorb the flavor of the filling. A fruit mousse, therefore, was best lined with fruity Roman punch, a popular frozen lemonade-like punch spiked with liquor and frequently used as a palate cleanser, and a coffee mousse with coffee ice cream. The simple ribbed melon mold was most common, but architectural shapes, realistic sculptural forms, and fruit and flower shapes were also greatly appreciated.

Most of the ingredients in the recipes that follow are fairly easy to obtain. Some fruits—especially gooseberries, quinces, and red currants—may be found only in season and in limited quantities. A few items—ginger brandy to add snap to cucumber ice cream—may require some searching at a specialty shop or gourmet grocery. I chose to hunt down cochineal, a powder made from the dried bodies of cochineal bugs, which the Victorians used as food coloring when they wanted a deep crimson shade. Eventually I found dried cochineal beetles through a mail-order craft shop (Earth Guild, 33 Haywood Street, Asheville, N. C. 28801; 1–800–327–8448); soaked them in warm water, then crushed them, adding more water, to obtain a strong blood-red liquid coloring. Strawberry juice, perhaps a more palatable substitute, is also effective, and fully authentic as well.

Each recipe here is authentic, reproduced as it first appeared in a nineteenth-century or early-twentieth-century cookbook, women's magazine, or cookery pamphlet—as it was used by Victorian wives. The individual notes that follow offer translation and clarification, all with an eye to remaining as true to the original as possible. In some cases, for instance, I've suggested increasing the amount of liquor used (perhaps temperance-conscious late Victorian cooks were somewhat sparing in that regard); in others, increasing the quantity of nuts or decreasing the amount of sugar or other flavorings, to taste. And throughout, for practicality's sake, I've advocated time-saving appliances like food processors, blenders, and electric ice cream makers—devices the gadget-happy Victorians would have applauded, and which affect taste to a negligible degree, if at all. Because the original recipe is printed intact, the choice of methods and ingredients remains your option. Remember on the whole, the recipes for Victorian frozen dainties are delightfully simple. They work as they were originally written, with little or no alter ation, and they work beautifully.

CHAPTER

1

Victorian

Ice Creams

THERE ARE MORE WOMEN WHO CAN FURNISH YOU WITH A GOOD ICE CREAM THAN A WELL-COOKED mutton chop, lamented Catherine Beecher and her sister Harriet Beecher Stowe back in 1869, in their guide, *The American Woman's Home*. And small wonder. Long before the nineteenth century, Americans adored ice cream. In the late 1700s George Washington, known for his discriminating tastes, purchased more than two hundred dollars' worth of ice cream from a New York confectioner and Dolley Madison was said to have awed inaugural guests in 1812 by serving "a large shining dome of pink Ice Cream."

It wasn't until 1845, however, with the invention of the patent freezer by Nancy Johnson, a New Jersey housewife—that ice cream descended from its status as a rich man's delicacy to a treat that could be savored in most American homes. (The machine was patented in 1848 as the Johnson Patent Ice-Cream Freezer by a William G. Young.) Prior to that, ice cream was made by the exhausting "pot method," in which the ice cream mixture (cream or milk, white sugar, flavoring, sometimes eggs) was vigorously agitated in a tin pot or pail for an hour or more, and simultaneously shaken up and down in a larger pot containing salt and costly pounded ice or snow. The ice-and-salt mixture brought the cream to freezing temperature. Cooks had to be diligent about scraping the semifrozen mixture from the sides of the inner pot and beating it well to prevent the formation of icy lumps, which could ruin both the consistency and the taste. It was a backbreaking and time-consuming process, in which the entire family had to take turns.

The new patent freezer, a mechanical hand-cranked affair with a churn and a dasher, reduced preparation time by almost half. Coupled with somewhat more affordable prices for former luxury items like ice, sugar, and cream (and the recent availability of extracts for flavoring) it brought the delight of a dish of ice cream within the reach of more people than ever before. By 1850, *Godey's Lady's Book* was able to declare no party complete without its serving of ice cream. "A party without ice cream would be like a breakfast without bread or a dinner without a roast," decreed the influential editor of *Godey's*, Sarah Josepha Hale.

Recipes for homemade ice cream proliferated. Manufacturers of freezers and flavorings soon joined with the intrepid sisterhood of Victorian cookery experts in creating all sorts of ways in which people could prepare and enjoy frozen desserts at home. Homemade ice cream was touted as far superior to the store-bought variety, which contained thickening substitutes like condensed milk and cornstarch instead of sweet, rich cream.

"Besides, it is often flavored with some cheap, rank extract, and it cannot be compared with the home made article. Try it and see," cajoled a booklet of recipes prepared by a Boston manufacturer of flavoring extracts and coloring pastes.

The patent freezer eased but certainly did not eliminate the drudgery of preparation. "Turn the crank for twenty minutes—not fast at first, but very rapidly the last ten minutes. It will be hard to turn when the mixture is frozen," Maria Parloa advised. The dessert thus remained something to be savored on special occasions—birthdays, family reunions, and the Fourth of July. In *Little Women* (1868), the March sisters were ecstatic at a surprise Christmas treat sent by Mr. Lawrence, their aristocratic and well-to-do neighbor, which featured ice cream—"actually two dishes of it,—pink and white." It was the wealthy Widow Douglas in Mark Twain's *The Adventures of*

Tom Sawyer (1876) who was described as regularly enjoying its consumption. "She'll have ice cream! She has it most every day—dead loads of it," Tom enviously maintained to schoolmate Becky Thatcher. And it was in 1908 that eleven-year-old Anne Shirley, the young heroine of L. M. Montgomery's *Anne of Green Gables* series, dramatically lamented that her supposed misbehavior prevented her from attending an eagerly anticipated Sunday school picnic where she would have the opportunity to taste—just think of it—real ice cream! "Oh, Marilla, please, please, let me go to the picnic. Think of the ice cream! For anything you know I may never have a chance to taste ice cream again."

Lemons, which were first imported in the early 1800s and quickly became one of the most popular flavorings for nineteenth-century cakes, pies, and puddings, also lent their tart tang to homemade ice cream. Other favorite early flavors included almond, strawberry, and vanilla. All kinds of fruit flavors, particularly orange, strawberry, pineapple, and raspberry, followed, and confectioners began to boast of the many flavors they offered. One, advertising in 1883, offered caramel, nectarine, filbert, apricot, plum, cinnamon, and currant among its twenty-two choices. Cloves, nutmeg, ginger, cinnamon, vanilla sugar, and maple sugar, along with extracts (almond, pistachio) and mint flavors like wintergreen, were also commonly used.

Although most recipe books advocated using cream, many Victorian homemakers prepared ice cream with milk, which at the time was rich enough. Arrowroot, cornstarch, flour, and even rennet tablets (one half to one tablet dissolved in each quart of milk) were often added as thickeners. Stirring in a small quantity of gelatin as a binder was recommended to aid in molding, to provide a creamy (as opposed to grainy) texture, and to prevent the formation of ice crystals. When no cream could be spared, Victorian cooks employed a recipe such as Mrs. Ellet's frugal "Mock Cream"—made by mixing half a tablespoonful of flour with half a pint of new milk, letting it simmer five minutes, then stirring the beaten yolk of one egg into the boiling milk, and running it all through a fine sieve.

Most food experts agreed that cake was the natural accompaniment to ice cream. "Send round always with ice cream, sponge cake: afterwards wine and cordials, or liquors [sic], as they are now generally called," advised Mrs. Ellet. Cookies and crisp wafers were also quite proper. But in 1903 Harriet H. Higbee, the principal of Oread Institute, Worcester, Massachusetts, included as one of her "favorite recipes of all recipes" the (then) innovation of serving vanilla ice cream with hot chocolate sauce—the sweet beginnings of a delicious tradition, a classic still enjoyed today.

ALL-PURPOSE VICTORIAN ICE CREAM BASES

꩜

Victorian ice creams begin with a plain, custardy foundation to which different flavorings are added before freezing. They are made plainer or richer by varying the amounts of eggs and cream to taste. The following three base mixtures were developed by Mrs. Mary J. Lincoln for one of the recipe pamphlets she prepared for the White Mountain Freezer Company in the late 1890s.

PHILADELPHIA ICE CREAM

Scald one quart of thin cream with one scant cup of sugar; or use one cup of milk with three cups of thick cream. When cold, flavor to taste, and freeze in three parts ice and one part salt. Very thick cream will not freeze readily. Scalding gives a firm, rich velvety texture, not found in uncooked cream.

CUSTARD ICE CREAM (FRENCH OR NEAPOLITAN)

Scald one pint of milk; beat yolks of from two to six eggs, with one cup of sugar; add hot milk; cook over boiling water till it coats the spoon; add a dash of salt, strain, and when cold, flavor. Before freezing, fold in the whites beaten till foamy, and add from one to two cups of thick cream, whipped.

Plain Ice Cream

Boil one quart of milk, or half milk and half thin cream. Mix one cup of sugar with two scant tablespoons of flour, or one of cornstarch or arrowroot; add one-fourth cup of cold milk, stir into the boiling milk, and cook twenty minutes, stirring frequently. Add two well-beaten eggs, and from one to four cups of thin cream, and sugar in proportion. Cook enough to set the egg, then strain into the freezer. Cool, flavor to taste, and freeze. You will not taste the starch if it is well cooked. When you have no cream use more eggs.

NOTE: Each of these foundations provides a rich, velvety ice cream base. The no-egg "Philadelphia" version is the simplest to make. The amount of sugar will vary with the flavoring (for the chocolate ice cream that follows, for example, sugar was reduced to ¾ cup). And, instead of 2 tablespoonfuls water (which adds ice), substitute 2 tablespoonfuls milk. The addition of eggs to the formula makes a custard base, which results in a richer ice cream of a smoother, creamier texture. Even today, a "French" ice cream such as French Vanilla denotes the addition of eggs and, thus, a richer texture. If you decide to try the richer, more custardy base, omit the egg whites. The "Plain" formula is the "inexpensive" ice cream (using milk thickened with flour, arrowroot, or cornstarch) that Victorian cooks made when they didn't have cream. This is surprisingly delicious, and tastes rather like an ice milk. It works especially well with berry flavorings.

BISQUE AND BROWN BREAD ICE CREAM

1 quart of cream
¼ pound of macaroons
2 lady fingers
¼ pound of sugar
4 kisses
1 teaspoonful of vanilla
1 teaspoonful of caramel

Pound the macaroons, kisses, and lady fingers (which should be stale) through a colander. Put one pint of cream on to boil in a farina boiler, add to it the sugar; stir until dissolved. Take from the fire, and when cold, add the remainder of the cream and freeze. When frozen add the vanilla, caramel and pounded cakes, and (if you use it) five table-spoonfuls of sherry; beat the whole until perfectly smooth. Pack as directed.

—Mrs. S. T. Rorer,
DAINTY DISHES FOR ALL THE YEAR ROUND, 1908

A model kitchen is every lady's delight.

—M. E. W. Sherwood,
THE ART OF
ENTERTAINING, 1893

NOTE: Bisque is an unusual and surprisingly tasty ice cream. Place ¼ pound macaroons, 4 kisses (a popular Victorian meringue cookie—see my *Victorian Sweets* for recipe, or substitute store-bought meringues), and 2 ladyfingers in a food processor and grind to coarse crumbs. Put 2 cups cream to boil in a double boiler; add 2 cups sugar and stir until it is dissolved. Continue with the directions as given in the original recipe, but chill the mixture before freezing. When it is almost frozen, add the remaining ingredients and 5 tablespoons of sherry. Continue to chill until frozen.

Makes 1½ quarts

For the Victorians' popular Brown Bread Ice Cream, use 3 slices Boston brown bread (made from a standard molasses flour recipe), 4 cups cream, and ½ cup sugar. Dry the bread in an oven, then pound and sift through a fine sieve. Continue as for Bisque.

BURNT ALMOND ICE CREAM

༈

1 quart of cream
½ pound of sugar
4 ounces of shelled almonds
1 teaspoonful of caramel
1 tablespoonful of vanilla
4 tablespoonfuls of sherry

Blanch and roast the almonds, then pound them in a mortar to a smooth paste. Put one-half the cream and the sugar on to boil, stir until the sugar is dissolved, then add the remaining pint of cream and the almonds; stand away to cool; when cold, add the caramel, vanilla and sherry. Freeze and pack as directed.

—Mrs. S. T. Rorer,
DAINTY DISHES FOR ALL THE YEAR ROUND, 1908

Mrs. Rorer's variations on nut creams:

WALNUT ICE CREAM is made precisely the same way as Burnt Almond.

For HAZELNUT ICE CREAM, eliminate the sherry and the caramel.

Make Filbert Ice Cream as Hazelnut, except do not roast the nuts.

Pistachio Ice Cream is made as follows: Wash 1 quart of spinach, throw in a kettle of boiling water and let boil rapidly for three minutes. Drain in a colander, pound to a pulp, and squeeze out juice through a fine muslin. Blanch and pound ½ lb shelled pistachio nuts. Finish the same as Burnt Almond, adding 1 heaping tablespoon of vanilla sugar or a teaspoonful of vanilla extract to mixture, plus sufficient spinach juice to color it a light green.

Note: This creamy ice cream, with its barely perceptible sherry flavor, has an unusually contemporary taste, but increasing the amount of sherry will enhance its nineteenth-century character. Roast ¾ cup blanched whole almonds in a 10-inch skillet over medium heat for 8 to 10 minutes; stir often so the almonds brown evenly. When they are a deep walnut color, allow the almonds to cool, then put in a food processor. Process 30 seconds, to a smooth, peanut-butter–like paste. Put 2 cups cream and 2 cups sugar in a medium saucepan over medium-high heat, stirring constantly until the sugar is just dissolved. Remove from the heat and add another 2 cups cream and the almond paste. Allow to cool completely. Stir in 1 teaspoon caramel, 1 tablespoon vanilla, and ¼ cup sherry. Transfer the mixture to an ice cream freezer and freeze according to manufacturer's directions.

Makes 1½ quarts

CUCUMBER
ICE CREAM

Peel and remove the seeds from the cucumber, and to
1 large-sized cucumber add 4 ounces of sugar and half
a pint of water; cook till tender. Then pound and add
to it a wine-glass of ginger brandy and a little green
colouring and the juice of two lemons; pass through
the tammy, and add this to 1 pint of sweetened cream
or custard. Freeze and finish as usual.

—A. B. Marshall, THE BOOK OF ICES, 1885

NOTE: Garnished with mint leaves, cucumber ice cream can be a
delicate and refreshing surprise at a summer luncheon. Three or
4 drops of food coloring give this dense, smooth cream an
appealing pale green hue. Instead of heavy cream, try a lighter
cream for a lighter taste. A tammy is a fine strainer, mesh sieve,
or wool straining cloth.

Cut 1 large peeled and seeded cucumber into rough chunks
and place in a medium-sized saucepan. Add 1 cup water and ½
cup sugar, and bring to a boil over medium-high heat. Reduce the
heat to medium and cook, uncovered, 3 to 4 minutes, or until the
cucumber is tender when pierced with a knife. Remove the
saucepan from the heat and allow to cool completely. With a
slotted spoon, remove the cucumber, put in a food processor, and

puree. Add ½ cup ginger brandy and press the puree through a strainer with a rubber spatula until all the liquid has been collected; discard the pulp. Combine the liquid, syrup, brandy, ⅓ cup lemon juice, 2½ cups heavy cream, ½ cup powdered sugar, and 3 or more drops of green food coloring. Transfer the mixture to an ice cream machine and freeze according to manufacturer's directions.

Make 1½ quarts

CHESTNUT
ICE CREAM

Use two quarts of cream, a cupful and a half of sugar, the juice and rind of an orange, a cupful of water, a gill of wine, thirty French chestnuts.

Shell and blanch the chestnuts, cover them with boiling water, and cook for an hour. Drain off the water, pound the chestnuts in a mortar, and then rub them through a puree-sieve. Put the sugar, grated orange rind, and water in a stew pan, and place on the fire. Boil for twenty minutes; add the chestnut puree, and cook for five minutes. Take from the fire, and add the orange juice and wine. When cold, add the cream, and freeze. The wine and orange may be omitted.

—Maria Parloa, MISS PARLOA'S KITCHEN COMPANION.
A GUIDE FOR ALL WHO WOULD BE GOOD HOUSEKEEPERS, 1887

NOTE: Chestnut ice cream has a full but subtle flavor, the perfect end to a festive dinner. For greater flavor, increase the amount of nuts used to taste (we used 1 cup coarsely chopped nutmeats).

Put cooked chestnuts in a food processor and process to a fine crumb. Put 1½ cups sugar, 1 tablespoon orange zest, and 1 cup water in a large saucepan and bring to a boil over medium-high heat; do not cover. Add the chestnut crumbs and stir with a wooden spoon until they have been absorbed into the liquid; do not overstir. Cook for an additional 5 minutes, lowering the heat if the mixture gets too dry. Remove from the heat and add ⅓ cup orange juice and ½ cup sweet white wine. Stir to combine and then set aside to cool. When cold, add 2 quarts cream, transfer to an ice cream machine, and freeze according to manufacturer's directions.

Makes 3 quarts

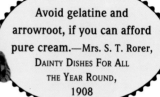

Avoid gelatine and arrowroot, if you can afford pure cream.—Mrs. S. T. Rorer, Dainty Dishes For All the Year Round, 1908

FRUIT ICE CREAMS

Put the berries through the press and use in the proportion of one cupful of juice to every quart of cream or custard. Sweeten to taste. Either canned or fresh fruit may be used, such as peaches, strawberries, raspberries, pineapples, apricots, etc.

All fruit creams or any frozen mixture in which a variety of flavors are used must stand to ripen and blend before serving. From two to four hours is the usual time required.

—Helen Louise Johnson,
The Enterprising Housekeeper, 1898

GOOSEBERRY
ICE CREAM

Put 1 quart of gooseberries on the stove in a pan, with half a pint of water, 6 ounces of sugar; boil, and when cooked pass through the tammy. If green berries, use a little sap green or apple green to color; if red, a little carmine or cherry red. When tammied, mix with a pint of sweetened cream or custard, and freeze.

—A. B. Marshall, The Book of Ices, 1885

Why is a pretty girl fond of ribbons? Because she thinks the beaux be coming.
—Open Secrets, n.d.

If you do not find it quite
acid enough to please your palate,
you can add in the strained
juice of a lemon.
—Frederick T. Vine,
ICES FOR SHOP SALE, 1910

NOTE: Gooseberry ice cream is tart, tangy, and flecked with bits of fruit. Colored with cochineal, it becomes a beautiful pale tangerine color. If green gooseberries are used, color with green food coloring instead of cochineal.

Remove husks from 4 cups of gooseberries and discard any bad berries. Put the berries, 1 cup water, and ¾ cup sugar in a medium saucepan over medium-high heat and bring to a boil. Reduce the heat to medium and simmer 2 to 3 minutes, or until the berries are soft. Put the berries in a strainer and push the fruit pulp against the strainer to extract as much liquid as possible. Discard the pulp, and set the liquid aside to cool to room temperature, then refrigerate until chilled. Dissolve 1¼ teaspoons cochineal powder in ½ cup water and stir. Set aside for about 1 hour, stirring occasionally, until the powder is totally dissolved and the mixture is paste-like. When the gooseberry liquid is cold, stir in the cochineal paste, 2 cups heavy cream (you can substitute light cream for a milder taste), and 1½ cups powdered sugar. Transfer the mixture to an ice cream freezer and freeze according to manufacturer's directions.

Makes 1½ quarts

CHOCOLATE
ICE CREAM

Make the foundation cream after either receipt, and whip one pint of cream to serve with it. Heat two bars of sweetened vanilla chocolate with two table-spoonfuls of water or enough to melt it. When smooth add gradually a little of the hot cream or custard and strain through a fine strainer or cloth into the remainder of the cream. If unsweetened chocolate be used, add two tablespoonfuls of sugar to it while melting.

Half a level tea-spoonful of Ceylon cinnamon may be mixed with the chocolate or half an inch of stick cinnamon may be boiled with the cream or milk; it gives a rich, spicy flavor. Or you may have another variety by the addition of one table-spoonful of caramel.

—Mrs. Lincoln, FROSTY FANCIES, 1898

Note: This is probably one of the best chocolate ice creams you will ever taste—sophisticated and not overly sweet, with a creamy, mousse-like texture. If left unstrained, it's flecked with chocolate bits.

Prepare Philadelphia base (page 18) using 1 cup milk, 3 cups cream, ¾ cup sugar, and a ½-inch piece of cinnamon. Combine 4 ounces semisweet chocolate with 2 tablespoons milk and 1 tea-

spoon vanilla extract in a double boiler over simmering water. Stir constantly for 3 to 5 minutes, or until the chocolate melts. Remove the cinnamon from the scalded milk and discard; combine the milk with the chocolate. Strain if desired; let cool before refrigerating. When cold, put in an ice cream machine and freeze according to manufacturer's directions.

Makes about 1½ quarts

CHAPTER

2

Water

Ices and Granités

WHEN THE VICTORIANS REFERRED TO THE TERM "ICES," THEY WERE THINKING OF A MUCH WIDER range of edibles than is suggested by its modern usage. The simplest, most basic form was the water ice, made simply from fruit juice and water, sweetened with sugar, and frozen in much the same way as ice cream. Prepared properly, water ices were light, clear, and fruity, and were often served at dances and balls, where gentlemen would be prevailed upon to bring "a plate of ice" for their chosen ladies.

Ices were also often served as palate cleansers during the lengthy formal dinners of the time—dinners that could last three to five hours. Mrs. Mary Henderson went on record as considering two hours quite sufficient, and noted with approval the dinner at Tuileries in which no fewer than twenty-five courses were served in a breathlessly efficient hour and a half.

On the other hand, a frosty water ice could also serve as a pick-me-up, especially when it was spiked with a liqueur or cordial. Favorite flavorings included Chartreuse, maraschino, kirschwasser, and noyaux—to which was added a little vegetable color to approximate the liqueur used.

According to a consensus of cookbooks, there were two ways in which to prepare water ices. One was to boil the sugar and water together to form a syrup, then cool it; the other was simply to mix the water and sugar without cooking. The former method was considered far superior, as using a syrup prevented the sugar from sinking to the bottom of the mixture, which, according to one late-century tract, resulted in a sharp, unpleasant taste. Another advantage was that the syrup could be made in large quantities, bottled, and kept on hand for later use.

The secret to making a successful water ice was that, once packed in the freezer, it had to be stirred only occasionally, with no need of the continuous churning with which one froze ice cream. Rapid motion would interfere with the clearness of the ice. This of course, necessitated much longer freezing times.

When fresh fruit or previously prepared fruit syrups weren't available, Victorian cooks substituted canned fruits (mashed and sifted, using the pulp as well as the juice) or melted fruit jellies. "While such ices are acceptable in an emergency, they are never equal to those made from fresh fruit," cautioned Mrs. Lincoln. They also had to be prepared with much less sugar. Even when preparing ices with fresh fruit, tasting the mixture before adding sugar was strongly advised, as fruits can vary greatly in sweetness.

The texture of water ice was comparable to that of wet snow—"more or less granular and icy, instead of creamy," said Mrs. Lincoln. A finer-grained ice was achieved by boiling the sugar and water until the sugar was clear, removing the scum, straining the syrup through cheesecloth, and, when it cooled, adding it to the fruit juice.

Victorian granités were half-frozen water ices to which whole small fruits (like raspberries) or cut-up larger fruits (like oranges) were added just after the mixture was frozen. The ideal texture was rough and rather icy. When a variety of different fruits were added the ices were called macédoines. As with water ices, granités must be frozen with as little stirring as possible.

> **If while opening a can of fruit or any similar thing, the juice should happen to spurt up in the operator's face, it is a good omen.**
> —HOME SECRETS, 1898

MACEDOINE ICE

Combine one pint of water with one pint of fruit juice and pulp—two oranges, two bananas, one lemon and grated pineapple. Make it very sweet, add a little salt, and freeze till mushy and remove the dasher. Stir in the froth from a pint of thin cream, giving a marbled appearance, and pack for an hour.

Other combinations of fruit may be used.

—Mary J. Lincoln and Mary Barrows,
THE HOME SCIENCE COOK BOOK, 1902

Very many times where two flavors are equally delicate, they give a pleasant change served together.

—Lincoln, Dearborn, and Barrows,
DAINTY DESSERTS, 1892

If you go to bed without cleaning off the table, the youngest in the family will get no sleep.
—HOME SECRETS, 1898

NOTE: This truly delicious, tropical-tasting fruit ice can be made with different fruits, depending on the flavor you wish to emphasize. Remember that Victorian fruits were smaller, and that fruit varies in flavor and juiciness depending on the season. The froth referred to would have been the extra-rich top layer of cream, which today, with homogenization, is no longer there. Therefore, the marbling is difficult if not impossible to achieve.

To prepare, squeeze oranges to make about ⅔ cup juice, remove the rind from a 1-inch slice of fresh pineapple, cut the pineapple into rough chunks, and puree it in a food processor to make about 1 cup pulp. Put 1 small banana and 1 tablespoon lemon juice in the food processor and puree to yield ⅓ cup. In a large bowl, combine 2 cups water, 2 cups fruit juice and pulp, 1½ cups sugar, and a dash of salt. Transfer the mixture to an ice cream machine and freeze according to manufacturer's directions. When the mixture is almost firm, stir in ¼ cup heavy cream and freeze 1 more minute, or until combined. The marbled appearance is very subtle, as the mixture is a pale yellow and the cream blends in quickly.

Makes 5 cups

LEMON WATER ICE

✥

4 large juicy lemons
1 quart of water
1 orange
1 ¼ pounds of sugar

Put the sugar and water on to boil. Chip the yellow rind from three lemons and the orange, add to the syrup, boil five minutes and stand away to cool. Squeeze the juice from the orange and lemons, add it to the cold syrup, strain it through a cloth and freeze as directed for water ice.

—Mrs. S. T. Rorer,
DAINTY DISHES FOR ALL THE YEAR ROUND, 1908

A VARIATION: GINGER WATER ICE

> 6 ounces of preserved ginger
> 1 quart of lemon water ice

Pound four ounces of the ginger to a paste. Cut the remaining two ounces into very thin slices and stir these into the water ice. Repack and stand away to ripen.

—Mrs. S. T. Rorer,
DAINTY DISHES FOR ALL THE YEAR ROUND, 1908

NOTE: This lemon water ice is sweet, not tart, and rather like frozen lemonade. Since nineteenth-century lemons were smaller, use 4 medium-sized ones instead of large, for ½ cup lemon juice, plus ½ cup orange juice, 2½ cups sugar, and 1 quart water.

Put 2½ cups sugar and water in a large saucepan and bring to a boil. Slice the zest from 3 lemons and 1 orange, taking care not to include the white pith. Add the zest to the syrup and boil, uncovered and without stirring, over medium-high heat for 5 minutes. Remove from the heat and allow to cool. Squeeze the juice from the lemons and orange, strain, and add to the cold syrup. Strain through a sieve or cheesecloth and transfer to an ice cream machine. Freeze according to manufacturer's directions. For the ginger variation, put ½ cup preserved ginger in a food processor and puree; cut the remaining ¼ cup ginger into thin, dime-sized slivers. Stir the puree and slices into the Lemon Water Ice syrup after straining it.

Both recipes make about 5 cups

STRAWBERRY GRANITÉ

1 pint of orange juice
1 pint of strawberry juice (from 3 pints)
1 quart of whole strawberries
1½ pounds of sugar
1 quart of water

Boil the sugar and water together for five minutes. Drop the whole strawberries into this syrup, lift them carefully with a skimmer, and place them on a platter to cool, then add to the syrup the strawberry and orange juice. Strain and freeze. . . . When frozen, stir in the strawberries and serve in glasses.

—Mrs. S. T. Rorer,
DAINTY DISHES FOR ALL THE YEAR ROUND, 1908

NOTE: The Victorians often enjoyed the rougher, icier texture of granités, which don't require the use of an ice cream maker.

Wash and hull 5 pints of berries; drain thoroughly. For juice, puree 3 pints of them in a food processor and place in a double thickness of cheesecloth to strain, squeezing the cloth to extract the strawberry juice (about 2 cups). Set aside. Without stirring, boil 3 cups sugar and 1 quart water in a large saucepan over medium-high heat. Drop the remaining 2 pints of whole berries into the syrup for 1 minute, then remove with a slotted spoon and place in a bowl to cool. Drain any syrup back into the pan, cover the bowl with plastic wrap, and refrigerate for later use. Stir the orange and strawberry juice into the syrup, and let cool before transferring to plastic tubs and freezing. When the granité is slushy but not quite frozen, stir in the cooked strawberries.

Makes about 3 quarts. This recipe can be halved if desired. (For an ice cream maker to function well, there should always be at least 1 quart of mixture. Recipes such as this one, which make large quantities, can be halved successfully.)

ROSE ICE

Wash a half pint of rose petals; pound them to a paste, adding gradually four tablespoons of granulated sugar. When smooth, add a quart of water and a pound of sugar, boil ten minutes; do not strain. When the mixture is cold, add the juice of four oranges strained through cheese cloth. Freeze carefully and serve in punch or wine glasses, garnished with fresh rose petals.

—Mrs. S. T. Rorer,
DAINTY DISHES FOR ALL THE YEAR ROUND, 1908

NOTE: This exquisite, fragrant ice has a translucent rosy, sunset glow and an odd, subtle flavor. Unless you grow your own roses (without spraying), prepare this recipe with rose water.

In a large saucepan, bring 1 quart water and 2 cups sugar to a boil over medium-high heat. Boil, uncovered, for 10 minutes; remove from the heat and allow to cool. When cold, stir in 1¼ cups orange juice, 2 drops red food coloring (or just enough strawberry juice to make ice a light rose pink), and 3 tablespoons rose water. Transfer to an ice cream maker and freeze according to manufacturer's directions.

Makes 1½ quarts

Red Currant Fruit Ice

Put 3 pints of ripe currants, 1 pint red raspberries, ½ pint of water, in basin. Place on fire and allow to simmer for a few minutes, then strain through hair sieve. To this add 12 ounces sugar, and ½ pint water. Place all into freezing can and freeze.

—Prof. G. Rudmani (late chef de cuisine of the New York Cooking School), Royal Baker and Pastry Chef, 1898

Note: When the Victorians didn't have fresh fruit on hand, they substituted preserved fruits or melted jelly, adjusting the sugar content as needed (see pages 34 to 35). We tried that method with Red Currant Fruit Ice and found jelly a worthy substitute in creating this sweet ice with its beautifully rich currant color.

Combine 6 cups currant jelly and 2 cups raspberries in a saucepan and simmer a few minutes, until jelly melts and raspberries soften. Strain through a cheesecloth and add 1 cup water. Transfer to an ice cream maker and freeze according to manufacturer's directions.

Makes 2 quarts

CHAPTER 3

Sherbets,

Mousses, and Other Delights

SHERBETS, FROZEN PUDDING, MOUSSES, RICH PUREES, AND OTHER FROZEN DAINTIES FILLED OUT the Victorian table year round, and homemakers were heartily encouraged to try their hands at these and other frivolous concoctions. "Don't be afraid of undertaking 'fancy dishes,'" urged Marion Harland in *Breakfast, Luncheon and Tea* (1875) as she blithely led her hapless readers into attempting all sorts of Frenchified dishes. "Sally forth bravely into the region of delicate and difficult dainties, when you are considering family bills of fare, and you will not be dismayed when called to get up a handsome 'company' entertainment," she chirped. Sherbets and mousses stuffed into bombes, frozen creams covered with meringue, and all sorts of other frozen desserts were the result.

Garnishes, not surprisingly, were an important consideration, particularly if the dessert was meant to be "a beautiful center-piece for the supper-table," as Marion Harland so frequently suggested. The fact that cooks were repeatedly admonished not to overdo garnishing, though, leads us to believe that garnishing often ran wild. Meringue was popular, and mounds of whipped cream were considered "a delicate garnish" for already rich frozen puddings and ice creams. Borders of greenery—smilax, parsley, and rose leaves—dotted with bright pinks, geraniums, verbenas, or roses were also employed.

Sherbet was made the same way as water ices, except that it had to be stirred enthusiastically during freezing and it contained egg whites, which accounted for its light, creamy consistency. "Care must be taken not to have sherbets too sweet, and yet they should be a little sweeter than would be agreeable if not frozen, as their extreme coldness deadens the sense of taste," advised Mrs. Lincoln in *Frosty Fancies* (1898).

Variations on traditional sherbet were also acknowledged. An extremely rich sherbet could be made with pure fruit juice and sugar (no water). Some recipes called for powdered sugar to be mixed with the egg; others for the boiling syrup to be poured slowly into the beaten egg and whipped until cold. Adding milk produced milk sherbet, known for its extra-creamy consistency. A tablespoonful of gelatin, soaked and dissolved, would give a sherbet-like consistency to water ice without added eggs or milk. All were served in fancy paper, small tumblers, or lemonade glasses.

A successful sherbet with a fine, smooth texture, but only half frozen, to which wine or rum or cordial had been added, was called a sorbet. (When made with citrus juice, sorbet became Roman punch.) It was served in glasses before or after the roast. Sherbets were eaten as dessert, but could also be served before the game instead of a sorbet or Roman punch.

"Frozen pudding" referred to a highly flavored ice cream or custard that contained fruit, nuts, and sometimes wine, and was often served with a sauce.

"Mousses" were light, spongy, chilled desserts made from flavored, sweetened whipped cream or egg whites and gelatin. Usually spread into a decorative mold, mousses had a rather feathery texture. "When it is cut into, its texture should resemble that of a fine moss found in the deep woods," described Maria Parloa. Although easy to prepare initially, mousses took a long time to freeze, often as much as four to six hours.

Parfait was usually a mixture of whipped cream, eggs, and flavoring, frozen in a mold packed in equal parts ice and salt, without being frozen. A frappé was a half-frozen, soft, somewhat snowy dessert, meant to be served immediately after it was made.

FROZEN PUDDING

(Furnished for this work by Mr. Sneckner
whose splendid Confectionery Establishment
is in Union Square, New York)

Cut up about half a pound of preserved fruits—such as peaches, plums, citron, raisins, and currants—add half a pound of Baker's chocolate, and a pint of best Madeira wine; simmer on the fire about fifteen minutes, and when perfectly cold add about one quart of vanilla ice cream. Freeze it in a two quart mould, and for the sauce whip half a pint of sweet cream flavored with vanilla.

—Mrs. E. F. Ellet, THE NEW CYCLOPAEDIA OF DOMESTIC
ECONOMY AND PRACTICAL HOUSEKEEPER, 1872

**Vanilla is the queen
of all flavors and shows to the
best advantage in whipped cream.**
—Lincoln, Dearborn, and Barrows,
DAINTY DESSERTS, 1892

NOTE: This special, very Victorian dish, served with a rich sauce fills the kitchen with a beautiful aroma. Because of the amount of liquid in this recipe, there are icy shavings in the texture, which give it an appealing nineteenth-century character.

In a large saucepan, combine 1 cup preserved pitted plums, ¼ cup dried currants, and 2 tablespoons candied citron. Add 8 squares (8 ounces) semisweet chocolate and 2 cups Madeira wine, and bring to a boil over a medium heat. Reduce the heat to low and simmer, uncovered, for 15 minutes. Remove from the heat and allow to cool before refrigerating. Once the mixture is cold, let vanilla ice cream (Plain Ice Cream, page 19) soften at room temperature 10 to 15 minutes, or until slightly softened. Stir in the chocolate mixture and turn out into a 1½-quart mold. When cooled, refrigerate until quite cold. Freeze in an ice cream machine according to manufacturer's directions.

Makes 1½ to 2 quarts

VIOLET SHERBET

Boil together for five minutes a pound of sugar and a pint of water, add the juice of two lemons. When icy cold add one pint of grape juice and freeze. When frozen, stir in a meringue made from the white of one egg and a tablespoonful of powdered sugar, and repack. Let this stand one or two hours to ripen. Serve in punch or wine glasses, garnished with fresh violets, or they may be garnished with the candied violets.

—Mrs. S. T. Rorer, Dainty Dishes For
All the Year Round, 1908

Note: This sweet, absolutely lovely grape-flavored sherbet in a brilliant shade of violet would be perfect served at afternoon tea.

In a medium saucepan, bring 2 cups sugar and 1 cup water to a boil over medium-high heat. Reduce the heat to medium and cook 5 minutes at a rolling boil. Remove the saucepan from the heat. Pour off ¼ cup of the syrup and set it aside. Add ¼ cup lemon juice to the saucepan and set aside to cool. When cool, refrigerate until cold. When cold, add 2 cups grape juice and place in the freezer. Once frozen, but not firm, heat the reserved ¼ cup syrup to 234°F. Beat 1 egg white, dribble it into the hot syrup, and beat until stiff, glossy peaks form. Stir the meringue into the softened sherbet and return it to the freezer to ripen overnight.

Makes 5½ cups

Maple Parfait

Beat four eggs, pour on slowly one cup of hot maple syrup. Cook over water till thick, stirring constantly. Strain and cool. Add one pint of thick cream, stiffly whipped, and mould for three hours.

—Carolyn Putnam Weber, DOZENS OF GOOD THINGS, 1915

NOTE: This is a rich, flavored whipped cream with custard added, and would be ideal as a cake filling. No ice cream maker is required.

Beat 4 medium eggs until light and frothy. Put 1 cup maple syrup in a small saucepan and heat over medium heat till hot. Dribble hot syrup into the eggs while whisking vigorously. Gradually add more syrup until the eggs are quite warm. Add the rest of the syrup and turn the mixture into a double boiler. Cook over barely simmering water, whisking constantly, until the mixture coats the back of a spoon. Strain, allow to cool, and refrigerate until cold. Beat 2 cups cream until stiff, fold into the cold mixture, and turn into a mold. Chill for 3 hours.

Makes 1 quart

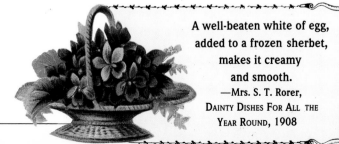

A well-beaten white of egg, added to a frozen sherbet, makes it creamy and smooth.
—Mrs. S. T. Rorer, DAINTY DISHES FOR ALL THE YEAR ROUND, 1908

CARAMEL MOUSSE

Use three quarts of whipped and drained cream, three gills of sugar, one gill of water, one of milk, two eggs, and two tablespoonfuls of gelatine.

Soak the gelatine in the milk for two hours. At the end of that time put one gill of sugar in a small saucepan, and stir over the fire until it becomes liquid, and turns a dark brown. Now add the gill of water, and simmer until the sugar is dissolved again,—it will take about fifteen minutes. Beat the eggs and the remainder of the sugar together, until very light. Put this mixture into the double-boiler, with the soaked gelatine, and the milk. Cook for five minutes, stirring all the time. Take from the fire, and add the caramel. While this mixture is boiling, pack a plain mould in salt and ice. Now beat the cooled mixture until it is frothy. Should it have become so cold that it is jellied before the mould is packed, place it in a pan of warm water for a minute, and stir until it is liquid. Now beat until it is frothy; gently stir the whipped cream into this. When the custard and cream are combined, turn the mixture gently into the mold. Cover, and set away in a cold place for four hours.

—Maria Parloa,
MISS PARLOA'S KITCHEN COMPANION, 1887

NOTE: Fluffier than our present-day mousses, this recipe is actually closer to a flavored whipped cream. Serve as a dessert with a crisp wafer or use as a filling for sponge cake. No ice cream maker is required. Put 2 tablespoons unflavored gelatin in a small bowl and soak in ¼ cup milk for 2 hours, uncovered. Then put ½ cup sugar in a small saucepan; heat over medium heat 5 to 10 minutes, or until it caramelizes. (As it begins to liquefy, stir the sugar to help it caramelize.) When the sugar is dark brown, add ½ cup water (careful, the caramel mixture will spatter a bit) and stir until the water is incorporated (it doesn't take the 15 minutes stated). Set aside. In a double boiler, beat 2 eggs and 1 cup sugar until this mixture resembles yellow ribbons. Beat in the soaked gelatin and milk and place over simmering water. Cook, stirring constantly, for 5 minutes, or until the mixture is heated through and the gelatin is dissolved. Now stir in the caramel and allow to cool completely. Pack in a 3-quart mold in ice and salt. When the mixture has totally cooled, beat the cream just until stiff and fold it into the mixture just until combined. Turn into the prepared mold and refrigerate for 4 hours.

Makes 3 quarts

APPLE SORBET

Two cups of granulated sugar, four cups of boiling water, one quart of sour apples, juice of two oranges, one fourth cup of lemon juice, one fourth cup of sherry wine, and three tablespoonfuls of maraschino.

Boil the sugar and water five minutes and add the apples cored and sliced, but not pared, and cook until soft. Rub through a sieve, and when cool add the orange, lemon, and sherry, and two or three drops of carmine coloring paste, to give it color. Freeze, as usual, using three parts of finely crushed ice to one part salt. When the mixture is partially stiff add the maraschino and complete the freezing. This will have a finer flavor if allowed to stand an hour packed in the ice and salt.

—Attributed to Miss Harriet L. Sheldon, principal of the Telegram-Union Cooking School of Bridgeport, Connecticut (WHITE MOUNTAIN FREEZER BOOKLET)

No wines are served with ice cream.
Ice water and ice cream seem to be quite popular combinations with Americans.
—Maria Parloa, MISS PARLOA'S KITCHEN COMPANION, 1887

NOTE: A cool, refreshing sorbet—a nice change from the usual tropical citrus flavors.

Use 4 small Granny Smith apples and ⅓ cup orange juice. Boil 2 cups sugar and 4 cups water for 5 minutes. Core and slice apples, then put in syrup and simmer for 10 minutes, until soft. Rub the cooked apples through a sieve and cool. Meanwhile, dissolve ¼ teaspoon cochineal in ½ teaspoon water and set aside for 1 hour. When the mixture is cool, add ⅓ cup orange juice, ¼ cup lemon juice, ¼ cup sherry, and cochineal coloring and chill. Place in an ice cream maker and freeze according to manufacturer's directions.

Makes 1½ quarts

PEACH BOMBE GLACÉ

Boil one quart of water and one pint of sugar twenty
minutes, add a scant teaspoonful of gelatine, softened
in cold water, and strain; when cold, add one pint of
peach juice and pulp (pared and stoned peaches passed
through a ricer or sieve), and about one fourth a cup of
lemon juice. Freeze, as usual, in a White Mountain
Freezer, and use to line a two quart melon mould,
reserving a portion for use later. Fill the centre with a
cup of double cream, beaten solid, sweetened with one
fourth cup of sugar, flavored with
one teaspoonful of vanilla or one
cup of sherry wine, and folded
into the white of one egg
beaten dry. Cover the
cream mixture

with the reserved sherbet, filling the mould to over-flow. Press the cover of the mould down over a piece of wrapping-paper, spread upon the top of the mixture and let stand buried in equal parts of the ice and salt about two hours. The cream mixture should be thoroughly chilled before being put in place. The paper needs to come out beyond the mould on all sides.

—Mrs. J. M., Hill, Expert Testimony on the Merits of the White Mountain Freezer and a Few Recipes, 1903 (Mrs. Hill's Favorite Recipes of All Recipes)

Note: This bombe is both delicious and beautiful to present—when sliced, there's a streak of white cream filling visible.

To prepare, boil 4 cups water and 2 cups sugar for 20 minutes. Meanwhile, soften ¾ teaspoon gelatin in 2 teaspoons cold water and set aside. After syrup has boiled, add softened gelatin and strain. When cold, stir in 2 cups chilled peach nectar, ¼ cup chilled lemon juice, and transfer to ice cream maker and freeze according to manufacturer's directions.

When frozen, line 2-quart melon mold with ⅔ of sherbet, spreading it a scant ½ inch thick. Set aside. Beat together 1 cup cream, ¼ cup sugar, 1 teaspoon vanilla or 1 cup sherry wine. Fold in 1 egg beaten dry. Chill. Pour chilled mixture into mold and cover with reserved sherbet, filling mold completely. Place a piece of wax paper on top. Freeze. To unmold, dip in hot water for 5 to 10 seconds. Refreeze for 5 to 10 minutes to firm before serving.

Makes 5 cups

BISCUIT PRINCESS

Ice cream colored and
flavored with strawberry
Cherries
4 yolks
¼ c water
⅛ tsp. salt
1 tbs. vanilla
1½ c heavy cream
2–3 c sugar

Boil sugar and water till it threads, pour over beaten
yolks, cook till it thickens, beat till cold. Flavor and add
stiff cream. Line melon mould with ice cream, fill with
this parfait mixture and cherries. Cover with buttered
paper, pack and let stand several hours.

—Carolyn Putnam Weber, DOZENS OF GOOD THINGS, 1915

NOTE: This special molded dessert—molded strawberry ice cream
stuffed with vanilla mousse and cherries—is really for experi-
enced cooks but well worth the effort.

In a medium saucepan, combine ¼ cup water and 2 cups
sugar. Bring to a boil over medium heat. Cook until the syrup
reaches 230°F on a candy thermometer, the "thread" stage.
Dribble the hot syrup into a bowl with 4 lightly beaten egg yolks
while beating vigorously with a whisk. Gradually add more syrup

until the yolk mixture is quite warm. Add the yolks to the remaining syrup and cook, stirring, over medium heat 5 to 10 minutes, or until the custard coats the back of a spoon. Remove from the heat and beat until cold. Add 1 tablespoon vanilla and ⅛ teaspoon salt and place in the refrigerator to chill. Meanwhile, put a melon mold in the freezer for at least 1 hour. When cold, let 3 cups strawberry ice cream (use Plain Ice Cream base, page 19) sit at room temperature for 10 to 15 minutes, or until slightly softened. Spread an even layer of ice cream in the mold about ½ inch deep. Line lightly with plastic wrap and return to the freezer for 1 hour, or until firm. When the ice cream is firm, whip 1½ cups heavy cream and fold into the custard. Remove the plastic wrap, turn the custard into the mold, and top with ½ cup (or an 8¾-ounce can) pitted dark sweet cherries. Cover with buttered waxed paper and return to the freezer. To unmold, dip briefly in hot water and invert. Freeze 10 to 15 minutes before presenting.

Makes 10 to 12 servings

TOBIAS,
FINE CONFECTIONS,
AND
ICE CREAM SALOON,
826 N. Tenth Street,
Parties Served.

Concordance
for
Modern Cooks

The recipes in this book were tested using a modern, electric ice cream maker, rather than an old-time hand-cranked machine, since we felt most readers would be doing the same. We used rock salt (which can be purchased in the supermarket) or coarse kosher salt.

In all cases, the absence of additives, preservatives, emulsifiers, and stabilizers allowed the purity and freshness of the nineteenth-century flavors to emerge. Of course, this meant that these ice creams had to be consumed fairly quickly, and few lasted for more than a week, even when covered with plastic wrap (to retard spoilage and the formation of ice crystals) and stored in the freezer. Water ices (made without cream) lasted longer, and certain flavors even improved as they ripened. Lemon, ginger, and mint, for instance, intensified dramatically within just a couple of days.

Victorian ice cream, as prepared with heavy sweet cream, is exceptionally, sometimes excessively, rich. Cooks today might prefer to substitute light cream, or even milk, which, in fact, the Victorians did themselves, though for economic rather than health reasons.

Despite the ease of making ice cream at home today—with the convenience of juicers, food processors for grating and pureeing, and the variety of readily available fruit—it's impossible not to appreciate the laborious effort that making ice cream once required. Compare the freezing time alone (about 20 minutes today) to the hours upon hours it took in the nineteenth century. Preparing our raspberry ice by wringing the fresh berries through cheesecloth (a satisfyingly messy, hands-on chore, red raspberry juice spraying all over) brought home just how difficult the whole process once was. Not only did cooks have to harvest and store the ice ("harvesting" required cutting large slabs of ice from a frozen pond or lake during the winter and keeping it frozen either in an icehouse or by burying it underground), and chip and crush it with an ice pick, but they, of course, always had to pick the fruit and prepare the mixtures, as well as boil up raw spinach to get green food coloring for making cucumber, celery, or pistachio ice, not to mention endlessly turning, cranking, and scraping the ice cream–making machine.

While Victorian cooks praised the new patent freezers —a vast improvement over making ice cream by the laborious pot method (see page 14)—ice cream making still called for a strong arm and a patient turn of mind. Hand-cranked patent freezers, of which there were many varieties (the Johnson, the Packer, the White Mountain, to name some popular models), worked by a simple churning method. The freezer consisted of a large wooden bucket filled with the traditional salt and ice mixture, into which a smaller, lidded canister for the ice cream mixture was fitted. Inside the canister was a stationary paddle called a dasher. As one turned an outside hand-crank, the blades of the dasher moved and scraped the freezing mixture from the inside of the canister.

Today, while wooden buckets have been replaced by plastic or fiberglass, and canisters may be stainless steel, the most popular ice cream–making method remains the same, except that the canister is rotated not by hand but by an electric motor. Since this method works more quickly, it tends to produce smoother, slightly better results. Some of these motor-driven models don't even require the use of crushed ice and rock salt, but only ice cubes and ordinary table salt.

All of the recipes in this book were tested using a ten-year-old electric ice cream maker by Waring. The process was effortless, though one must be sure to monitor the machine, as the ice around the inside canister can get stuck and needs to be adjusted from time to time. The entire procedure takes about 20 to 35 minutes.

Another new, easy-to-use ice cream maker is the Donvier type, consisting of a hollow metal canister with a special coolant (when you pick up the metal tub, you can hear it slosh). Before using, you must chill this machine in the freezer compartment of your refrigerator for at least 8 hours. You then remove the canister, fill with the ice cream mixture, cover, and crank every few minutes till the mixture is frozen (usually just 12 to 18 minutes).

Ice cream makers such as the two described above are reasonably priced (under $45) and readily available, and represent the two most common methods today. Refrigerator-freezer units that are placed in the freezer compartment of your refrigerator and plugged in through the closed door (a motor churns the ice cream mixture) also exist. While they have the advantage of not needing salt and ice, they are far less readily available. Freezers with self-contained refrigeration units are perhaps the easiest method of all—you simply pour in the mixture and turn the machine on. They produce a smooth, superior product because of the speed with which they freeze. Their drawback: price, usually several hundred dollars.

A note on storage: Ice cream should be stored in covered, airtight containers, with a piece of plastic wrap placed under the cover to help prevent the formation of ice crystals. But these precautions are short-lived, as homemade ice cream should be eaten within a day or two after it is made.

HELPFUL HINTS ON MEASUREMENTS

30 drops	1 thimbleful
60 drops	1 teaspoonful
1 dessert-spoonful	2 fluid drachmas
1 tablespoonful	½ ounce
1 wine glassful	¼ pint
4 gills	1 pint
2 pints	1 quart
4 quarts	1 gallon
63 gallons	1 hogshead
84 gallons	1 puncheon

—DRINKS A LA MODE, 1891

ACKNOWLEDGMENTS

To Grace Young, Joanne Leonhardt Cassullo, Marie Luise Proeller, and Deborah Geltman; enthusiastic tasters and testers Thomas Cohen, Stacy Leopold, Estelle Leopold, Spencer and Justin Leopold-Cohen, and Michael Young; for design, Mary Wirth and Beth Tondreau; to Barbara L. Sollers and to Allan "Mr. Ice Cream" Mellis, for their generous contributions to the visual material that appears in this book; and especially to Lauren Shakely, Kristin Frederickson, and all my talented friends at Clarkson Potter—my thanks.